To Paint A Thought

Treena Humphrey

BookLeaf
Publishing
India | USA | UK

Presentation by *BookLeaf Publishing*

Web: www.bookleafpub.com

E-mail: info@bookleafpub.com

ISBN: 978-93-5744-460-6

First edition 2022

DEDICATION

For mom and dad.

Thank you for always supporting me.

PREFACE

Imagine what the sky would look like at night if it were to be more colours than just black.
Would it be like the aurora borealis, or like something that words cannot even begin to piece together?
This is an exploration of things that we know, written as though they are something that we don't.

To Paint A Thought

What does it mean
To paint a thought?
You could quite literally paint it,
In picture form,
Still life of a moving image.
But that wouldn't really
Do it justice,
Would it?
The millions of details,
Small things that
only you can see.
So maybe to paint a thought
Means to let go-
Surrender the details
That want to
Hang back the most.
But then again?
Maybe that's still too complex.
And maybe you
Cannot truly
Paint a thought.
But you can
Paint a picture,
Paint with words, or with ink.
So that's some place to start, Right?

A gift, I feel

I was asked:
"What moment did you love the most?"
It had been a long day; I didn't respond for a beat.
"I cannot decide," I responded eventually.
"Why is that?" My friend asked.
"Because each moment is a gift, and how could I love any gift more than another."

absolute beauty

The sky.
Have you ever seen anything filled with such
emotion before?
The colours of a sunrise,
the sky becoming awake.
Yellows and oranges, a pink blended well.
It's a morning for the sky as much as it is for us.
And the sky does cry;
Absolutely filled with tears, raining down to
drench the earth below.
A cloud filled with endless grey, bringing along
a flurry of frustration.
Then the canvas will be painted,
pink and purple light reflecting along clouds to
create a different momentary dream.
And like us, the sky sleeps next; recharging for
the next day of feelings ahead.

A Night With The Knights

Never had I thought that I would be sitting amongst a bunch of knights in a darkened room, seeing a film about the final duel that was ever recorded in history.
But that's just that,
That's what we did.
It was just us-
A full row to ourselves,
spread out to fill our comforts.
And someone would make a comment,
which caused unparalleled laughter from the rest of the group.
The energy amongst us was something made of pure comfort.
And even after the movie,
as we left,
we were engaged in each other;
We were present.

thunderstorms part I

You either marvel
or fear in
what you do not know.
A lightning bolt could strike
and send a shock of
every emotion through your body.
But you aren't really afraid
of the lightning,
are you?
Your fear
stems from
Yourself.

A New Career

I could have labelled
my nerves to my chest,
their journey down my spine,
and through the expressions
that I did project.
As the waft of red wine
from a freshly spilled bottle
expanded across the room.

A new career at a place,
so central to the human taste;
and I marvelled in the inclusion.

Each person I met,
brought a story so vivid
to my mind;
And I tried to remember a time
when I never felt so at home.

Characters

Every inch of the world is
An expression of personal form,
Warping together too create
A figure of ourselves,
An example of creativity
In its excess.

Each body owns a mind
of particular taste and a
View of this moment as they see it.

And upon meeting someone new
In a setting unending,
Ever changing; it is a way
To create an image
Of how hey are and how to do seem.

Because you explore someone's character
Is to know how they work,
A clock of the human habit
That ticks in the stability of time.

Manifest

This day I started to test
A practice so commonly
Passed around.
A single word- manifest-
Has been spreading a wildfire
Like a popular song.
So in the morning I began,
Opening my mind like a flowing spring;
To the idea of this new
Way of thinking.
I am and I will and I can.
Processes to bring you up,
To bring energy to your body.
By the law of attraction I learned how
To trust in myself;
To finish the story.

Unfinished

The ending was left open,
So quickly cut off at the base
Never to see the path that they would take.
None of it made sense,
A word here, a caress there of the
Gentle heart that knew nothing and of
The healing one who new much.
They were never to finish in the storybook land,
For their fairytale drew ever too quickly to a
finish.
And if the prince never loved the princess could
the villain win her love?
For the villain, misunderstood,
Made a mistake that shook he whole tale.
And he failed, every one knew,
And the prince took the princess
With the dragon laid slain.
The fairytale with an unfinished ending,
Waiting to be opened and completed again.

Walking Down

These steps are a lot.
Concrete, lined with yellow.
I could walk down them-
But I don't think I could run.
What if I trip and fall down?
What if I slip and then crash?
These steps are too long, too many.
Do I need to get to the bottom anyway?

The yellow is a caution sign,
A reminder of the pain that I could endure,
of the terror that could come.

So maybe I'll stay at the top;
Won't step foot over that line,
Won't walk down them too quickly-
only if I have to.
Cause at the top it's light,
And the darkness trails at the end.

These stairs are too many.
I think I should not travel them again.

thunderstorms part II

Rain peaks down to the roof below,
an expression of lightning,
the thought of fear.
And the leaves of each tree,
blows like a whisper.
The storm is supernatural,
a work of fiction ever binding,
a fear of the natural world.

The roof can only
bear so much weight.
The trees can only
withstand so much wind.
For the storm isn't
a cloud of fluff and tears;
But the deep down anxiety
that spreads from your chest to your eyes.

You're frightened;
This storm is inside.
A power raging through your veins
until the lines break

and spark and flicker.
The storm let’s on.

How are they defined between love and lover?

A love is about connection, physical, emotional. A sensation that understands each other on feeling and in mind.

Moments, words, actions- little things that mean 'love' in more ways than just intercourse. An intimacy made more than just touching and feeling but in understanding and adoration. That is the way to define a love from a lover.

Noir

Trees tower higher than her,
her feet barely touch the ground.
She runs, her breath heavy;
It mixes with dirty air.
The darkness of the moon
revives every inch of her soul.
Whispers fill her ears,
they cloud her vision
and take over her mind.
The whispers,
thoughts long since forgotten.
She is plagued by them;
Her hands sink into the moist earth.
Electricity flows through her veins
and explodes as if from wires-
into the ground.
The thoughts fan out,
expanding into the sky.
The thunderstorm crackles on
I'm the ever expanding dark.

That's How The Story Goes

It's not always about the words that are said,
Or the way they are spoken,
Rhymed or delivered.
It's sometimes about the moment,
The content,
The energy.
A specific passion within the encounter,
Something doomed to fail or succeed
At the beginning
Or the end.
And she could have sent him
A list of songs,
But he would listen to them.
And he could have told her
All of his thoughts,
But she would still not understand.
Because words are funny that way.
As they either connect,
Or fail to give reassurance.
And that's just how the story goes.

She Tried To Understand

The situation from afar
looks sheltered, clouded-
But it's not something that's
supposed to be understood.

A person so in love,
so driven for a character
that will never be theirs.
A arm, just out of reach,
for another pulls it away.

The other contains love;
An overwhelming understanding
for the persons aching heart.
But it is the ignorance
that wells up
and drives the person to
aim the arrow
and release to separate
the pair from one another.

It’s a push and a pull

of want versus gain,
and they go back and forth,
between who means what
and where the love
is really destined to remain.

As Wind Is To Fire, They Are Doomed To Fall

All that the wind could ever want is the earth.
But she is overwhelmed with the desire to what
it would feel like to kiss the fire.
And the wind could never ask for any one thing
else but the earth,
But fire's force and his unanswered story pulls
air to relish in what could be.
And all she finds herself desiring
Is the flame.
But a fire, no matter of how great or small, could
ever be a match
for the force of the wind.
And with a blow for a kiss, and fire's own
curiosity to submit,
his flame blew out;
Their story of a love lost
left only to play on loop
as the wind dances sadly
through the trees.

The Blue Knight and the Green Knight

It was more of a feeling between the two of
them.
A mutual hate brought on and simmered below
the depths.
Of course, that's not how every story started out.
For they both fell for a princess,
Sat so close at the tournament.
She was their fairness, their reason to win.
But a foes hate could never subside,
When the love of the maiden is won,
And the victory rightfully attained by the green
knight,
Paved way for the title to change.
For fairness and all of the green knight wit the
maiden,
The blue knight set to plot his revenge,
A challenged left in the handbook of time,
A duel to be victorious with chivalry and luck
for one.

Frozen In Time

We talk a lot about painting,
about a brush stroke across time-
and we stop in a moment,
frozen, untouched.
A group of friends, yet strangers-
communal around a table.
Simple, momental.
All talk is held back, drawing-
it's like they are waiting for
a topic to surface.
But the drinks arrive
and the conversation opens up to
gossip and relating talk.
Open air and the spice of food;
A moment as though laced
through an enjoyable loop.
And the final strokes are added,
the conversation warming up,
ideas melding together.
The last details to accent the art
fine line every memory created in the space.
A night coming to a close,
simply finished, and the painting
lays complete.

Silence's Problems

The silence had problems with following rules.
It never came when it as needed
And allowed noise to penetrate through
At the moments when it was deepest enough.
And then it would force a famous awkwardness-
When the air asked for a laugh.
The silence never came when I needed it,
Because it had no control
Over the noise in my head
That I had succumbed
And relented to.

Like The Seasons

Petals, blooming;
wilting, falling;
un-lasting, ever-changing.
Our love, changes-
Like the seasons-
Blooming, wilting,
seeding.
It comes and goes,
and is always growing,
like winter into spring-
or dying like summer
into fall.
We are in an endless cycle,
like the seasons.
Our love bound to
grow and then die
over and over again-
until the end of time.

like a picture, like a sound

And so the canvas dries,
a melody of crimson and violet,
dancing across the greenest fields.
A cloud swirling of cotton candy bubbles,
expanding and breaking apart-
like the surges to your mouth,
or bubbles to a bath.
And as a song sits upon the surface,
the melody winds along the branches of
the story, the touch to be reached
for up and through the canvas.
I'll say that this thought
is a memory, painted by a song of sweet speech,
Remembering a one time summer romance;
Left to be only a melody.
So I'll paint this image,
drowning it in my own words,
carving it with a silver pen.
Then I will step back and take a glance
at the illustrated thought
now forming in your mind.

www.ingramcontent.com/pod-product-compliance
Lightning Source LLC
Chambersburg PA
CBHW051759130826
49812CB00033B/1205
9789357444606